LOUDER PRAYERS

SEVENTY-ONE POEMS

LOUDER PRAYERS

WRITING TWELVE

PETER HAGUE

LOUDER PRAYERS
Seventy-one poems

First published in 2022
by Peter Hague Concept Design Art Direction
www.peterhague.com

ISBN 978-1-8382746-6-5

Cover Design, layout, typography, photography
and cover art by
Peter Hague Concept Design Art Direction.

Also available in hardback: ISBN 978-1-8382746-7-2

The author's opinion on the artistic ability of Damien Hirst
is not necessarily correct or shared by others.

A catalogue record for this book
is available from the British Library.

Also by Peter Hague

hope in the heart of hatred
Twenty-nine poems

gain of function
One hundred and two poems

summer with the gods
Seventy-three poems

Remembered On A Frozen Breath

I live near the sea

and the sea shouts over the hill at night,

using its laughing voice

to scald the air with healing salt.

The garden is frost and the moon is bright.

I dedicate this quiet truth of cold and night

to everyone – as promised.

A Welcome

Welcome to my words. To some extent this book resembles an earlier anthology of my work entitled 'Gain of Function', with its reliance on new poetry, some of it first published on the internet. Yet it also has a strong relationship to my previous volume called 'Summer With The Gods' – where this new book asks for 'Louder Prayers' combined with a further search around the edges – those still unexplored areas not quite touched on before. It is certainly a further development of my writing style, and although its physical presentation is designed to give the feel of a prayer book, it is an honest proposition and not in any way disrespectful, sarcastic or facetious.

I have tried to make this book as readable as possible and to this end there are no overly long poems. It is constructed in five parts – in the hope that these considerations will make the reader more able to follow the thread of poems in the order they are placed, which has some value regarding the way I construct my anthologies in all their disciplines myself, believing that to be an important part of their final creative presentation. It also provides some interpolation between the various poems, and in some cases helps them lend support to each other. Once again, in accordance with my investigation of style, it is a book that takes my poetry to new levels and is a reading of souls; an observation of ambition; a release approximating that of mercy; a desire for philosophical communion – but not least, it is a true entertainment made of thoughts, feelings, experiences and words.

As said, much of the work is relatively new, while other poems have been in revision for quite a few years. There are three poems that were published first in 'Anima Poetry' in 2017-18 and others published in 'Fevers of the Mind'.

Those readers aware of my work will notice that once again I have included a handful of pictures, and although these are given more prominence than the ghosted impressions I have used before, I still maintain that they are no more important to the message in the poems than their forerunners were – as previously explained in other volumes. They are applied only to support the mood of the book as a whole.

Another strength of these poems is a legitimate need to touch on a number of social issues – coming at them in abstract ways. Since I do not favour any political or social leaning, there is no attempt to sway the reader. Yet I feel my observations, political or religious, need at least to be aired – or what's the point? In no way is my work an exercise in demonstrating pc notions or pseudo-religious guidance, but words must be allowed to identify potential problems and quasi current situations in a critical or merely heuristic sense.

INDEX OF POEMS

Louder Prayers - book one -

MERCY

Louder Prayers - book two -

COLOUR MY SHOES

Louder prayers - book three -

HOPE SURVIVES

INDEX OF POEMS

Louder prayers - book four -

BOY BLUE

Louder prayers - book five -

A PAGAN PAGEANT

LOUDER PRAYERS

Louder Prayers –
Book One –

MERCY

1:1

Mercy

I am in a room with Roy Orbison.
All the girls are looking towards him;
wondering if he is blind or in hiding.
I am so obscure I don't even know him.
So obscure I don't know myself –
whether I am an accident of obscurity
or an achievement of reluctance?

It is my turn now – let me be glorious –
let me write a structure using thousands of words.
Let me build a poem that stands like a cathedral.
Let me write a lotion of impeccable language –
smoothing words into chapters and prayers,
and on, into the skin of a pretty woman.
Prayers will forgive her perfection of form –
they know who she is – and not just pretty –
she is a woman of forgiveness and considerable mercy.

Let me impress her with my unknown head –
speaking unknown words into the evening air.
Let me desire her – using a cult of words
purposely stolen from a nightclub in Soho.
Let Roy Orbison endorse my work.
It won't make any difference that he's dead.

The Man Who Haunts The Town

When I leave my attic I am threatened by dust;
it haunts the staircase – drives me back.
Yet I always make it through this storm of nature;
this ghost of unwarranted physical intrusion.
The last step fools its careful eye,
as I slip out of sight – into pagan streets.
And I am soon on a yellow bus to a golden store,
where I buy more provisions to keep me inside.
I am always glad when the dust is healed
and locks my door.

I am happy in this attic with its notebook and pencils.
I store them in a fridge so my writing is dispassionate.
I am a cold man – a relic of the north,
whose mother was kind at cheering him on.
I mostly write about unnerving experiences
with unworldly captors, made of dust;
who never state their full intensions –
or care for the identity of the wretched host.

I am the man in the dressing gown;
I am the soul who haunts the attic –
and sometimes –
the man who haunts the town.

Home Is Where The House Is

If I were a house
I would stay at home.
Even when I was out on the town,
denying rumours
of my reclusive tendencies.

1:4

Hallelujah Anyway

I can't make it to the church today,
but hallelujah anyway.
Use my blessings where you can.
I understand the holy plan.

I lost my way in youth and lust.
I lost my hope in broken trust.
I can't make it to the church today,
but hallelujah anyway.

1:5

Damien Hirst Is Not An Artist

Damien Hirst is not an artist;
he is a technician.
Technicians are artists,
but only during working hours.
If technicians become unemployed,
then they become artists –
but only until midnight and never at weekends.
If guitarists become technicians
they too become artists
and they all watch snooker
with their snooker player friends.
Good friends win championships –
rolling in on guitar riffs,
and are not just technicians – they understand flare.
They can smell success in their deep sharks' water.
And have the fabulous nerves
of unrecognised artists.

A hymn to the genius of Ronnie O'Sullivan

1:6

Past Forward

The shock of the new
is rivalled by the shock of the past,
that bludgeons all contenders
and fabricates its future.

It develops a clean status –
polishing filthy boots –
calling itself 'history'
on the walls of museums.

It relies on the expectations
of eager formality
and also the blunt rhythms
of current institutions.

First published on Twitter – 2 September 2021

Peace

A skein of geese crossed my path;
high in my window and heading north.
I was on a treadmill – ebbing into the future;
moving like a time machine –
moving like a V shape.
Peace.

1:8

Lyrical Sundown

English country graveyard.
Hosting Eleanor Rigby.
Blackbird singing to the dead,
in the night?

1:9

Expecting No God

Little by little the stars are closing in –
winking out their simple light,
to grow the sky into a fire of feathers –

a fearful thing –

firing-up the furnace of our being
and of our final spring.
As we crawl out from earth –
dead and empty-handed
but with wings.

A Milkshake Meets The Milky Way

Has the sea finally taken him out?
Shaken him out, beyond its foam –
to float a while in the smoothest pleasures
of azure blue and peacock green.
Colours, even this northern sea treasures –
and can be seen, settled into
on quiet afternoons.

It lingers nearer the shore in summer,
looking for ice cream or a living creature –
the sea has always been a subtle killer,
and draws in life as if drinking from a straw –
becoming comforting, like the breast of a mother,
or a tempting thing – an endless treasure –
always one step away from misadventure,
or the tidal places where we will rest in eddies.

We refuse at first, but the sea is a door
with a lift-shaft descending to a shifting floor,
where all manner of things are fashioned from sand,
and its destructive patterns, devised aeons ago.
It is devoid of hatred – just a little solemn:
a self-bereavement by mechanical action,
yet with an underlying need of reckless death

in order to sustain a churning entropy.
It is the survival of waiting for an unsure breath –
the sense of finality, we all know well.
It guides everything to its proper path –
even under the sea's alluring swell.

We all have our waves to meet and embrace –
they move our lives into the next true shallows;
the parts of the future where our shadows are cast,
best and strongest, upon the cosmological rhyme.
We beat as a pulse in the universal paradigm –
a greater god than that fashioned by religion,
or any priest has declared sublime.

1:11

The Clock Is Coming

That we are only here for a short time,
we must do our good, greater than our wrong.
For we are only here for a moment of theatre,
then gone.

Schubert's Unfinished Heart

So soft those fingers played us in –
a gentle skin of unwinding wind;
uncanny in the language of ivory stutters,
yet never blowing
through an orchestra's breath.

An impromptu arpeggio,
musing Beethoven's respect –
a fellow, who recognised a similar song.
It was the window of deathbeds,
where the future continues –
and where everything passes,
yet all is unfinished.

To the unfinished memory of Franz Schubert.

1:13

Shopping With Anne Boyd

In a modern art and crafts arcade?
Or a 1930s wainscotted room –
and why not?
She would kill the gloom
with her soft avalanche
of bohemian beauty.
For shopping with Anne Boyd
is an enchanting pleasure –
I focus my astronomy on her starry hour,
where our careful negotiations
involve only our spirits,
and where everything is lost now,
becoming unredeemable.
Like that moment we sat on her painted bed –
a warmth made of sunlight immersing the room.
A comfortable silence – on the edge of embrace.
Yet stirring the nothings of beautiful fools.

The Eye Of The Needle

My soul says I am becoming too much to bear;
there are too many demands on my life and work
for me to seriously, actually care.
I have betrayed my soul by simplifying life
with templates and patterns –
with queues and strings.
I need to free myself from this burden of shallows –
get to locating the scheme of things.

I have become spider-like, with many legs
and each leg testing this sparse arcadia –
and with as many eyes, or maybe more,
though these are mostly blurred – or unkindly sure.
They wrestle, unfocussed, with the daily tensions
that gather in the square root of ceiling to floor.

I cannot keep up with myself anymore,
or the clock of weeds that has grown around my chair.
I sit beneath the square of an unchallenged pyramid,
where the weight of its stone, threatens the most –
resting on each one of my feet – and more –
and who knows how many hooves or claws or toes?
I am flattened by the mountain of many years;
the climb has become obsessively steep,

'The Eye Of The Needle' continues...

and the vertical lines arch back in atonement,
where all my fields have an inhibiting slope.

There are many unanswered and stark propositions,
and things half-forgotten or left too late.
But it is not a matter of heart or duty,
or even the clinging conscience of dependant fate –
that brave substance by which we rally to survive,
and which rolls us on, like a wheel of fire.
It is deeper than that and more contrived –
it is the subject of debate in each parliament soul.

I sieve for the truth through my many ashes,
as I am crushed by the gravity of weak assumption.
It is a weight measured in the pain of inches,
and I am one step above the glorious avalanche –
the heroic fall I know God has determined.

I once had time for a simple back-burner –
a place of thought and steady consideration,
but now everything seems wasting and scarce:
no fuel in the generator – no horse for the hearse.
My life is like a shoelace, permanently undone –
cast out from the galaxy of its spiralling birth –

yet still attached to my eager response,
while flung beyond the light years of knotted dance.

It is a loose-ended universe that trails its purpose,
but never sincere enough to gather stars.

I need to find a way to put a lid on my life –
to bolt it down – but not gasping for air –
not the oppressive foot of a pyramid's square,
but a crude torpedo or a thundering rocket,
storming its way to the brilliant high-heavens.
A ship that will carry me – painless to the future –
a loyal soul – grateful –
passed through the eye of a needle.

A safe, sealed vessel made of nourishing sleep.

1:15

We, The Ascending

We can but know the future,
so that it offers its gift of life
by minding the past.
By knowing our own history
before it waves itself away.

Close in on your story as it escapes you
and you will broaden your knowing;
you will tease out your fate.
Expand your wings beside your falling,
cupping the reasons you earnestly worked for –
seeding the possible with every enthusiasm.

The larks rise and we rise with them.

Amen to you who listen to me –
in your past and future –
in your lost days and your light.
Here is the path – waist high in corn –
head high in summer,
in the drying wind.

You will need to smile to gain its attention
and walking as we do, between corn and thorn,

we witness our civilised work – to completion;
tending the world in the light of itself,
and in a city's streets of crumbling convention.

The larks rise and we rise with them.

Wherever you find your light is your mission:
abiding God's great challenge of wary creation.
With a lifting narrative, sung at midday,
weeping into the cupped palms of every true story.
And also in that moment, before deliverance,
when we cannot speak, lest we carelessly betray.

The larks rise and we rise with them.

Louder Prayers –
Book Two –

Colour My Shoes

2 : 1

The Mask Becomes A Smile

o not worry, you are safe in our hands.
This poem is not a claw
aimed at your guilty conscience,
or a threat to your existence
in a soured neighbourhood.
We are not 'The Outer Limits'
and are not concerned
with controlling every aspect
of your next hour.
We leave that to you,
while offering an embrace
and the added encouragement
of a firm handshake –
a random display of plausible humanity,
yet both practical devices
to fill an episode of the above.
For we have heard tales
of engineered and mutating viruses –
and offer love.
We also offer a badge of honour,
gifted in the form of a trusted mask –
awarded at a safe distance and with a printed smile.
For if ever humans needed the art of levity,
it is in this last mile.

2:2

All People Die Of Redacted Hearts 1

What is living? This fixed twilight?
Time will soon have its toll.
All the best words are redacted now,
so abandon your poetry for the hills of song.
Let go.

Songs are redacted by populism and fear:
so bring your redacted words over here!
We will lay them on the couch
and mend their language;
we will rewrite your involvement
in devilish folklore.
We will starve the redacting pen of silencing ink
and blot out its testament of abolished words.

So cast your novels to the writing wind;
they need the harassment of awkward weather.
Cast them on the troubled beauty of the sea,
before the old folks – made vivid by their memories,
die long before lovers – and of redacted hearts.

Death Leans Into Laughter

The worst part of approaching life's end
and seeing the prospect of death
stalking your shadow,
is when they start to move the scenery
well before you thought of going.

Yet the future becomes much less progressive
and not the place you imagined it to be –
tampered with, would be a better confusion –
for planning has no substance
without an anchored soul.

Besides, you can't help but accept the hint –
and in many ways it is time to go;
there can be no future
if the transcending revolution
is merely annoyance with truth,
led by postmodernist denial.

2:4

Rebellion Is A Structured Culture

The virus will always kill itself
by reinventing itself anew.
You cannot learn to live with a virus
that is learning not to live with you.
You cannot get ahead of a random stride –
there will always be a nought point two –
hiding in a lab of human soup –
common as a bloodstain in the human zoo.

This particular virus is a natural force,
even if concocted by a human hand –
nature's revenge is inclusive of idiots –
a concept we will come to understand.

June 2021

Here And Astray

Cats are the gatekeepers
of uncertain windows.
You can see it in their eyes;
they are beyond glass.

2:6

Imaginary Healthcare

Why experiment
with the whole population?
Herd immunity?

Haiku 5/7/5 syllables

 First published on Twitter – 16 October 2021 – Haiku

2 : 7

Silent Witness

All digital now.
The press rusts in a corner.
Words go unprinted.

Haiku 5/7/5 syllables

The Neophyte Poet

After five years of commercial art
the patented student returned home.
Caught in a blessing of new horizons,
yet not implored to walk or crawl or jump
between an old and rising sun.
The winding road was uneasy with its miles
and being too long, had come undone.
And I, not needing threshold or milestone
to imagine new worlds beyond each gate,
my task was to find another form of study –
to investigate – or at least to find its simple gold,
shimmering lost, in the stream of intentions.

I let these formative lectures come unto me –
imagined in my head while I sat in the garden;
drinking symbolic vermouth, or usually tea –
listening to Beethoven through his billowing staves.
Music was indispensable then,
and it was there, under that listening sky,
beneath that nothing bowl of blue,
that I, listened to the rambling soul of philosophy too,
and the various implications of its impeccable quest.
I also pondered its extensions of literature
and none of this seemed to stray into pretence.

It was just reading the magic of Rupert Bear
in all the tiny stories of mankind's thinking.

I had begun to write poetry during my years away,
to offset the lame art of bland commercialism.
I wanted something real – and writing seemed okay –
it filled the void around me
with the detail of stone and air.
Every human concept has a cloud of dilemma;
in every living thing, or singing field.
I could not point it out then, it was just too loud –
either in Tennyson's crannied wall
or the branching of a tree.

And in all these garden years I practised the craft
I even studied depression and its paramour – torment.
It proved a pleasant subject while the sun shone bright –
it was like checking the guide ropes of a perfect tent
while still exploring the other side of night.
I wanted to understand the explicit truth of things –
although relaxing in the garden
was never far from right.

2:9

Seasons Are A Time Machine

I met myself today – sitting in a garden,
or in some prayer along the way.
An ambitious sun –
steaming the clouded words astray.
It was a blue smothering of stiffening light,
yet I, called upon by north and night, said:

> *"Winter will soon shrug us, like a careless deity –*
> *swept without mercy into houses of blight."*

For now, the blanket sun simmers our tales –
of here and there – and of yesterday.
My two safe selves, a returning continuum,
with a winter shift beginning to blow.

And travelling the lawns of memories and summers,
in different gardens of yearly flowers,
with buds yet unopened and words unsaid,
an echo will sound from those spilling hours.
Some circular notion that hardly turns –
a lingering condition of the seasonal array.
Another north of bleak and bitter words
my returning self will be compelled to say...

The Edge Of Exile

Depression has wrung out all my instincts.
I am standing outside my work,
which is a bad idea.
I really can't bear to live this moment
without my yarns and poems
and their neutralising hour.
A glorious gathering of notions and tides,
with their various controls
and explanations.

Yet I have a surplus of experience, ready to hand –
enough to cast this slippery fish
further into the vile, black pond –
a glimmering lure that attracts the eyes
of the murderers and writers who occupy those deeps.

These scribes of torture, who own so many deaths,
will soon taste a swallow of their own gruelling pain –
squeezed from the sluice of an unknowable reservoir,
with its poisonous prayers and a pity of life.

Colour My Shoes

These are the death days – disease,
instability and resentment
are creeping beyond the controlling slight of hand;
rolling outside suspect human measure.
We cannot hold back the spread of our folly
or the demands of our pleasure.
And as insanity itself, our tainted blood is shot
with the genetics of an energised decay –
punching blindly out of the isolating tower;
stretching to reach our quarantine of bedlam.

Obsessed by numbers, we count our oblivions:
labelling death with the belief of science –
that great sham of parody and ultimate cliché
that answers our questions – at great expense.
Our conceit is to outnumber beast and bird –
sending them knowingly to a precious death;
leaning on the false virtue of obliterating reach,
with the confidence of vanity, never tailing off.
We record their demise with a marketing smile,
blessed with the apology of sundry charities.
It is the beautiful wrapping of emblematic sweets –
offering brazen respite from their brutal lives –
or from other brutal beings – always part-human –

that murky variant we are compelled to shun.
They swim in the pit of human slime
and are not included in our scheme of civilisation.
There is no multicultural rainbow for militants;
they are carefully forgotten in a fog of convenience.
Or banished from the neighbourhood –
considered an error –
never corrected or said out loud.

Our planet is crazed with anguish now,
and is trying to reject us from its daily routine.
Our 'unwanted' poster is in every town hall,
but we have no shame to beg for civil mercies.
Instead, we accept Earth's unimaginable stress,
pretending to subscribe to a pale shade of green,
as nature sours under our deadly breath –
falling with the centuries, to its broken knees.

Our expanding population has found new ways
to explain its numbers – to demand more seats –
to abolish the resentment of greed and money –
reducing communications to the limitations of tweets.
The so-called elite, swim in sly silence,
making poverty kneel to their selfish schemes,

thus trapping mere tenants in a homeless distance,
trailing their cogs from a corrupt machine.

This pile of broken bones – too late for knitting,
bends with our weight on the splint of contradiction –
the simultaneous spreading of cure and disease –
we are crazy with the industry of lunatic bees.

We have made insanity our beast of burden.
It is the only animal equal to the task.
See it hitched to our back, like a saviour's saddle,
lost in a momentum that will not rest.
The rainforests are filled with the ghosts of trees –
soon to be camouflaged by leafless death.
It is a creaking planet of withering faith,
with a need for castigation well beyond gods.

Our streets are caked in the usual ambivalence,
where progress is represented by colourful shoes –
they are aimed to catch the misery of human vision –
its eyes cast down into its human blues.

Louder Prayers –
Book Three –

HOPE SURVIVES

3 : 1

Something Certain

nd I am starting out
with a need to go home.
It is early in the sky
and darkness prevails.
Light is tuned-in
for the eagle eye.
Yet we see nothing lurking
in the compromised shadows.

Night will breakaway,
challenged by our mood,
as trees draw the darkness
into new shades of mono.
We are walking in summer –
there's a hole in the road –
autumn is stored there.
We will be brown tomorrow.

Hope Survives

We can't keep breaking our world
and expect to live in unbroken cities.
We cannot live beyond darkness and squalor
if we drench our light
with mistrusted ideologies.
Down in the basement, beyond all our dreams
is a room made of wasteland
and piles of lost luggage.

   First published on Twitter – 17 October 2021

3 : 3

Cold Witness

Watching every horror from birth,
the Moon made its night
into an endless orbit.
Cold as it was,
out there in the silence –
not wishing to witness
more than a single day of Earth.

3:4

The Tolling Bell

Every day, I wake up depressed
and in the mouth of pity.
This goes on for at least two minutes;
just enough time for a suicidal death?
Maybe not long enough to write the note?
Yet every day I wake up dressed in pity –
every day I wake up in depressed mens' pity.

Suicide's alternative is to pour a coffee –
let the day bloom – to find me out.
My thoughts will gather in the folds of dreams
and fall back into the fads of living.

The 'tolling bell' is never a game I play –
where humans gather for death's scant insight.
I am taking my depression to a safer edge –
one that casts my being into the size of a forest.

I will be lost in the expansion
of depressed mens' souls,
yet I will wake with the choice
of being a leaf in autumn.

Cryptic Virus

It is with a heavy heart
that I decline
the covid-19 vaccine.
I will not die
with some tampered genetics
coursing in my blood.

Unless, of course,
I die of the virus instead –
as awarded with the functions
of its laboratory murderers.

February 2021

About my concerns with gain-of-function research.

3:6

Louder Prayers

There is always enough intrigue
for experimentation.
Yet we are as children,
playing with an extendable virus.
It will understand our every working,
and declassify our secret words
before we even inject a sentence.
It is playing us like a plague –
see it glisten – our new invention.

We have set the world a-twirling
and there is no rest position.
Yet there's always room for tampering –
for louder flavours beyond our prayers.
And we all know God's not listening –
but has passed our fate to an insulted Earth,
who uses our lust for vanquished enemies –
and performs a trick of sly collaboration.

The soul and spirit of Earth rejoice,
in the resulting darkness of illumination –
this riven biology of a fooled humanity,
and the revenge of genocide
by an outraged planet.

  Human kind is also a tool of nature's control.

3 : 7

Death Disrupts Its Own Reduction

Death needs a party to survive.
There is no death
without struggle and embrace.
Death is merely a time-out,
waiting for the knock
that slams a door in a particular face –
the knell – not called for, or justified,
but neither out of place.

It is the black – in the white paint of life
that finally dulls the sharps and flats
to hear out the essential mysteries of grey.

You shall have your garden of Eden, yes,
but only at the end of a fully traversed day.
And expect the light to dim your dreams
into the closed bud of impotence.

The Fish-Eye Lens Of Death

You cannot see the world
without some form of distortion.
It wraps around your head mysteriously –
half of it unsure
and held only in memory –
it is a second gone by
and anything can happen,
especially in that blind spot
of unnecessary coordination.
You cannot see the world
from any other place than where you are,
even with technology –
certainly not –
that would always be suspect and unsure.
It would likely be awash with trickery and invention.
No, you cannot see the road behind your back,
or those leaving as you turn.
The world makes you nervous that way –
makes you squirm,
until you rest in the fish-eye lens of death.
Then, with closed eyes
you are blind to nothing.

     First published in Anima Poetry – Issue 4 – 2017

Walking On Water

If I could walk on water, would I be a fool

to think it was more than just tears beneath my feet?

That kind of skill never leads to very much,

like magic – its praise is never quite complete.

It will always seem a trick to some

and you would never gain their trust.

A true messiah would be an ordinary man,

whose wisdom leaves such elaborations out –

especially potential feet of rust.

If I were walking on water now,

I would be standing in a similar room,

on a similar street, in a similar gloom,

with a similar, tear-stained carpet at my feet,

and the warm blood of my own grail

hidden in defeat.

This carpet is a map of things to bear,

with ripples instead of wear and tear.

I could distract myself and dance with castanets.

I could allow fishermen in to cast their nets.

But I would probably move myself on then

and start the process once again –

to summon an angel with a single click…

or just to hang this dripping carpet out

and beat it with a stick.

Three Dark Hours

A poem is a word
made from all words;
made from all hours
and all the many minutes.

Made from a sea of creatures,
and from fingernails,
and from insects
and the breath of sparrows.

Made from horizons
and their span of expression,
where our thoughts linger
amongst the smallest truths;
amongst the stretched words
and the smallest wisdom
that represents nothing
but the puzzle of place.

Here are the words
we reduce down to whispers –
a pile of lost thoughts,
in fragments of letters.

These are the moments
that retain their darkness;
where poems are labels
to an unyielding silence.

And the sum of their existence
in the totality of being,
amounts to nothing more
than three dark hours.

"Into your hands I commend my spirit."
The last words of Jesus on the cross.

3:11

The Long Years Of Poems

Fifty years ago I found a garden,
beneath the static compressions
of a welcoming sky.
And inside the sound-pool of insect lore,
they translated life's business
into the shortest words –
their scarab words,
that only beetles and moon moths may ignore.

These are not my first years of poems;
it has been a long journey
from north to south;
from those tides of belonging –
to where I am now,
in this entirely dubious and nocturnal beginning.
I lit poems in the dark, to light my way;
their wax is still with me,
crusting the decades.

I have a life of poems – a popular history –
a diary of my most troubadour days.
They are blessed with a clarity you may not expect
from the frosted depths of a seeming malaise.
Yet I have seen beyond its clouds and fog and rain.

I still light these poems now;
they are a flame that never goes away.
And years of poems later,
they all have their particular thing to say.

Yes, I still light these candles in the dark –
they are made of who I am –
a translucent wax – a Peter Pan.
In some uncharted future,
they will blow through my tomb –
a life's waking whisper
in a moth's favourite room.

The Body Stops – Yet Hope Survives

With the sea behind me
and the land folding back into my life,
there is never one conclusion,
or one way to finish this.

The body stops – yet hope survives.

Twenty Years By A River

I have spent twenty years by the side of a river,
in a village that has an endless flow of ghosts.
A seasonal flow, like the river itself,
and with a daily ebb-tide of circling humans.
They soon slide as flotsam back to the swirl
of their own local streams and stifling eddies.

I weary in an eddy of my own making –
washing dishes in the back of a haunted teashop;
avoiding the plague-like utterance of denial,
or the nagging voice of the telephone.
This village, in its limestone crack,
is not a backwater, nor a central haven.
It is a transient stream of entertainment –
we provide a service and do not look back.

Eventually though, we are inevitably stuck;
this beast of entrapment will not let go –
this village of tentacles and snagging claws
is always a net for passing fools.
And although there are good reasons to prolong our stay,
some emotional and some mysterious,
most are uncertain, as melting snow.

'Twenty Years by a River' continues...

The genuine reasons to leave are obvious,
and if you really want to know:
we should run from this village – it burns the soul;
it breathes with a painted mouth of fire and veneer
and there is no peace in its false paradise
of circus sawdust and the smell of lard.

The village is a place of brutal fantasy –
it fools itself while trying too hard –
its mythical beasts perform as rats,
and there is a giant octopus in the river now.
I saw it gloating in the soft yellow gloom,
where its knotted form becomes a persuasive tool;
an unravelling ploy, sent to wrap our doom –

...and I feel a tentacle now, around my leg,
begging me to stay and promising joy –
and it is also tightening, like a noose,
yet with a friendly voice calling: "ahoy!"

I am suddenly moored here – an empty vessel,
with the old pissed-pants of a cracked hull.
I have become a warning buoy, in rusting yellow,
rolling against my chains, like the ghost of Marley –

I am clanking with the energy of my dear dead friend –
an eternal knell, who hung his own fate.

This river is a history – a clock made of water;
not quite flowing in sync with time.
It is seemingly interminable –
it makes things longer –
it stretches lives out like rubber bands.
In truth, the river is always leaving –
running like a thief with complete indifference;
smearing the village with an endless gloss –
a village of old men – made of nothing.

The limestone doom of Betjeman's climbing,
still bears thin witness of Bethesda's congregation.
His high yellow attics – exhausting in summer,
have no calculated cool in Siloam's shady rill.

And even an octopus cannot wrestle the minutes
or the relentless flow of currents or tides.
So in desperation it clings onto us
with its tentacles of temptation and suicide.
I have spent twenty years by the side of a river,
counting the harvest of blossoming pilgrims.

To Matlock Bath and pilgrim Betjeman.

Out In The Estuary

I have the mind of a swollen river.
It has become brown and dirty these days –
scrubbing at its banks with a rebellious message;
whispering with insidious lips.
It keeps me awake and makes no sense –
washing at the roots of established trees,
but I will not sign up to being part of the sea.
I am a river – and between these falling shores
I have set myself free.

I will languish in mud and bide my time,
with an old, broken boat and other debris.
I have an enlightened opinion of my rippling life
and let it pass into the blur it must be,
but I will not follow that dilution into the sea.

I need no details of waves and tides
and have come to a halt in a soothing sludge.
I am the torrent of spring that never was –
I have seen too much and blessed it by.
And I am frozen like Lot's wife – looking back –
at the clear, fresh water of new beginnings –
yet undeniably tasting of salt.

 First published in Anima Poetry – Issue 5 – 2018

Louder Prayers –
Book Four –

Boy Blue

4:1

Boy Blue

tay away from politics.
You won't change the world
but it will change you.
You will become disenchanted.
You will become too rigid to hear the truth –
you will become blue.

Truth will receive your payments
for being used as a lie.
You will deny the truth
without worthy hesitation.
You won't change the truth
but its spirit will leave your heart.
You won't change the world,
only how you perceive it.

Your world will be blue.
Your blue will be red.
Your heart will be yellow.
Your soul will be dead.

What's Left Of The Media

Democracy and equality are noble fools,
but need none of the bluster of foolish games –
crafted videos, featuring plight and hunger,
armed with visits to the pandemonium of war zones.
This dark agenda of 'transmissionary' scripts
seeks to tease the swelling of our ambivalent oceans;
seeks to move us from the confidence of dollar trust
and the safe, spanning ribs of our glorious ships.

But democracy has built its abiding tools,
and has welded a bulkhead of worthy dominion.

So although traitors are tolerated in a left-wing cabal,
being happily skilled in the reddest of weather,
there will be no rescue by collaborative media –
their comrades stepping back to watch them wither.
Cohorts fear the march being stolen from beneath them,
or their microphones yanked from their wiry veins –
apologist tones will be cast into the judgement –
with a rebalancing of words on their current position.

Some tears of mercy will sweeten forgiveness,
while a voice in an earpiece ends transmission.

4 : 3

Active Intolerance

Symbolism is everything –
a question of perception.
If you can get some fool to kneel
toward a disguised revolution,
then you have won the foolish game –
but have lost the trust of fools.
They will take back their gift of ignorance,
leaving a doubtful celebration.
You will have darkened the perception
of a trusted common sense.
You will have enslaved your own misery
inside an altered history,
where everything black is random –
and all things white are liberal.
And truth is forced to balance,
where not one word is neutral...

then there's your own ambiguous statue
you will need to pull down.

4:4

The Changing Hand Of Socialism

The weak tea of socialism is a strong brew these days –
a dangerous brew, with no truth in the bottom of its cup.
Once profound and respectable, it is a corrupted idea,
made of weeping facades and a comrade media.

They have borrowed the jackboot of fascist thinking;
now softened with the polish of devoted hypocrites.
An appropriation excused by their allied reporters
and laced by a lip's-worth of altruistic pledges.
If you do not agree with all they say
they will dust you down with labelling words –
divisive accusations made of stale critique,
mashed too long in a cracked pot.

They are uttered in a darkness of moralising mouths –
those self-appointed clerks with cancelling tongues.
They roam in the libraries, among serious statements,
yet condemn true words in an arrogance of suppression.

Social forbiddance, used to render change,
is a dangerous thing in a bandit hand.
Or hidden in the fingers of an iron glove,
that has started to smash
the ornaments of its neighbours.

True socialism has been bled by mercenary rogues –
stealing ammunition from its funding benefactors.
They will vouch for the intention
that props their existence –
a gloom beneath the shutters of a golden lie.

They pretend to be experts in every field –
those of ancient worlds and topical religions.
They are students of dilution and altered scriptures
that stain dark in the truth of ordinary light.
Such miracles as embedded in the Turin shroud –
that other vague tea bag of wavering notions;
steeped in ambrosia to prolong its image;
wrapped in the zealous faith of eager proof.

They gather similar plaudits from an elevated silence,
claimed-pure with a stirring of milk and honey.
Or the blusterings of men, with demands and offerings –
the three kings lurking under high moral ground.

Faith is ranked bottom in their casket of gifts,
as they feast their intentions on communist crumbs –
denying their part in 'the bread and circuses';
demanding change from whichever hand it comes.

4:5

Episodes Of Silence

It is enough that we have nothing to say.
Lay down your lips and remain aloof.
The station here, has its talented trains,
but the wind will take you to the next town.

There is hell here in the broken city –
and the skyline is tempting, with its long delays.
There are stories on the horizon that are never told,
they are written in dust, then blown away.
Send all your literature to our crowded air –
we will pretend we are civilised
and breathe its values.

4:6

Song Of The Cavemen

Sons are in fear of their fathers.
Fathers in fear of their ghosts.
Everything and all things are measured in loyalty –
no need for an abundance of threatening peace.

Run to the hills with your powerful stones;
you cannot be masters in the peace of cities.
Take all the equipment and ammo you were given –
maintain the ghost-fighting in the bitter hills.

You will not succeed in a true leaders' war –
you will always be hampered by a warlords beginnings.
And as the West turns away a beleaguered blind eye
you can continue your campaign of belittling women.

August 2021

4:7

No Haircut For Old Men

There is no haircut for old men,
but the haircut for young men
will shape their youth –
a military cut – short back and sides –
a common thing, suitably hypnotised.
A trending lifestyle of denied privilege,
with the alluring mirage of exotic words.

Sixteen barbers on an English street,
each mystifying a global trance –
a foreign fare of international trends,
wounding the patch of indignant police.
What do they expect from a country of nothing?
A place without nurture for muzzled young men,
whose ancient grandfathers did all the fighting –
but beyond short back and sides
nothing was won.

4 : 8

Poker Face Towns

There is no bro – only terms of courtesy,
cast in the clichés of a modern full house.
Or in a hand of cards, dealt in diversity –
far too suspicious for the slow eyes of poker.
We are flushed with pride and deal straight words,
but are usually hampered by additional jokers.
Yet the North is too jaded for diverse comedy –
and the discomforting woke of a discordant South.
And it's too late for howdy – too cold for truth –
too hard to even say hello.
And there is no bro –
for we have too much mistrust in betrayed little towns
for their borrowed chips to be cashed out loud –
so we say nothing – merely mumble in the crowd.
And there is no bro – only another displaced Joe;
waiting like a sacrifice at the factory gates.
They are chained with foreign locks now
and sealed with mistakes –
and an unclear status of friend or foe.
Joe is our delegate – a bought pioneer –
he smothers the smoke of viral fireworks
with rumoured wealth and a Chinese New Year.

From a conversation – overheard

4:9

Silence Is The Birth Of Intolerance

The first gas lamps had a welcome shine,
though they never were a friend of mine.
I always liked the dark lamp, down the street –
where shadows swam like tadpoles around its feet.

The gaslight you refer to now
is darker than the darkest crow.
It extinguishes truth with feathered words,
while plotting sparrows tweet your way –
pointing down into the darkest dark of a deep decay.

The gaslight now is a form of oppression;
an exploited trust of unnecessary delay.
The gaslight now, glows without mercy;
far into a night-time of unabridged silence.

Time Being, Is A Difficult Place 2

What is living? This fixed twilight?
Poems say nothing because no one listens.
The news is uncomfortable
and is grown from agenda.
What is this living that betrays its cohorts?

To avoid misunderstanding
the best words will be redacted.
Soon we will listen only to unlit pages.
And these worst words will underpin
the utterings of salvation.
They will be uncomfortable reading
when society flounders.

Abandon all poetry for the hills of prayer.
Abandon all prayers for the skill of whispering.

Say any words with no god listening.
Say any words with no god laughing.

Play host to the chequered memory
of sanctified meaning,
in this redacted mood of twilight and terror.

Somewhere Becoming Mundane

Be careful, there's that politician guy.
Soon he will be trying to talk us down,
or kissing your baby – with a breath of beer.
Insisting there are more lyrics in Beatles songs
than we normally hear.
All this is to gather your weak indulgence –
and glue your phone to a mobile influence,
as he paints his colour on your passing face
and announces how wonderful the policemen are.
He will burden your skill with failed ideas –
saying they failed because you are lacking in purpose.
He will stuff failure into all our pockets,
doling it out while shouting forgiveness.
Suggesting the Country is "unsafe in our hands;"
employing migrants to queue on the beaches –
scaring up embedded, indigenous instabilities –
training a future to be cold and unforgiving.
"The workforce will be more enthusiastic soon,
with new slaves, slipping past voter ignorance."
He says this – winking a devious eye
and firing arrows into the brilliant air...
seeding foreign workers into an energy of slaves –
somewhere becoming intolerable;
and later mundane.

4:12

The Pool Of Self

If I could weep this mask into a pool –
the dripping face of a designated fool.
I could set my sentry eyes
to the stoic care of unravelling nature;
give them a confidence for guarding horizons
with sweeping gestures and squint expressions.
I could set my hand to boil some water,
for the formality of tea between each prayer.

I am hoping for rubber boots and green overalls:
brilliantly stubborn and bred on farmland.
I want to add substance to the thickest plot,
always keen to patrol the limp countryside.
I want insanity as wide as a grin –
or as subtle as the menace in a heaving tide.
I want the mercy to begin.

Sometimes we have to be as cruel as nature
to see things through to their resting place.
But also to find, within our deeper selves,
those watery depths – overwhelmingly appealing –
shrugged by gods, yet loved beyond question.

We have governed this false map too long,

'The Pool of Self' continues...

with furtive winks and glorious signs –
they deal death to so many things,
trusted to the paper of dying trees.
We sign this treachery with invisible ink,
on the disfigured pages of unripened poems,
and sometimes by colouring the paper safe:
with disarming shades of green or pink.
No one is fooled by the human sin
that wants to reach behind the rules.
That wants the mercy to begin.

The excitement of nature is ready to reply,
whereas I am worn-out and ready to die.
And I just want darkness now,
or just the light of a tiny goodbye.

I will crawl inside an unexploded bomb
with my imaginary god and a temporary tomb –
some world war relic at the bottom of the pond,
which I dug in good faith with my deepest hand.
And where my nature blurred its softest water
and formed this human from unnatural blood.
I will be ready to hatch out soon enough:
into someone focussed and unquestionably good.

I will exist beyond the shallows of tepid science,
where lies are released in the unravelling of knots.
And there is no need of response or uncertainty,
or to powder the scene with forensic dust.
I will be one who knows no slavish spectrum
and can breathe the visibility of its broader chart.
For the whole universe is an infinite eye,
and it is wise to rise above human blindness
before we peer into its fabulous skin.

We could of course, scribble our fragile name
at the point we want the mercy to begin.

And we will not be expected to wear a facade,
such as the annoying beauty of a human face.
There will be no hidden portion of daily lust –
and no dry footsteps to distract our seconds.
Our watery path will be set to listen –
to hear within ourselves, the silence of love.

4:13

Seasonal Betrayal

It looks like autumn is not working for me.
Each time I embrace it,
she moves into winter.

4:14

Sand Castles

I spy with my youthful eye
something beginning with sea.

A Paper Path

The best sense of freedom fills the heart
while crossing a country road
between indifferent hedgerows –
a blue sky afternoon underpinning our trust,
where the undecided game of death
is the business.

A solitary car goes by in a breath;
we are returned to the mesh of singing birds;
and the loose-ends of insect flight, wired to the Sun –
who can tell if they know their course – they might?
I hear tell the bees know more than most
and draw maps in the form of dance.
But there is no sun-dance here today,
in spite of a relic plane, ignoring our parade:
a Spitfire distributing its high, loyal song –
threatening no one – vain as a lark.

Nonetheless, death is the business.

We are intruders here, and each moves as a cog,
picking at the stillness of a summer peak –
first-footing across the order of a stitched line of paint
that speaks to travellers in a broken code.

Its desert of tarmac builds a wild edge –
more a lost instruction than a certified road;
a feathering of scorched grass and tumbled grit.
One could almost feel unthreatened here,
but opposing freedoms are always attacked –
mostly by the greed of agent fools.
They feed off the practicalities of human needs
and laugh in the face of honour and trust.

There is no war here, but fear is the business.

It sets us walking like a clockwork wind,
and there are many millions of us following behind:
many millions to fill those countless spaces,
where footprints stray into a promised land,
tapping their feet in a persistent drone –
the traditional mapping of the way, is gone.

The new billions – the bone souls of the south,
have wrapped the world with a bitter ease
and tipped their lives on the seesaw of adventure –
with globalism poking a rod at their backs.
It is a spoon of promises – stirring the longings
of an unsustainable and broken home.

'A Paper Path' continues...

It pretends to know each wandering soul:
acknowledging the pirate commerce of staying alive.
It is that springboard of the disparate south –
their perceived armies in a north-bound trek;
longing for the rich hemisphere of delicious living –
that rumoured feast, awaiting guests –
All fooled by a falsehood of new beginnings.

There is no war here yet, but death is coming.

The northern grail is marked with dotted lines;
awkward on paper – signed with smiles –
and the ephemeral strokes of easy politicians,
in their ecstasy of exercising borrowed power.
They have miscalculated the call for human brotherhood –
that eventual stain in the pockets of traders.
They thought words were the mortar of written walls –
a handshake and a wink, between old competitors,
but they were visible to the longings of a drowning world –
tapping restless feet with a morse-like code.

They came on foot, crossing dotted lines,
to exploit the naïve heart of northern latitudes –
to feel the pomp and circumstance of justice

and its limited capacity for worthy outcomes.
What did neophytes care for lines of surrender,
drawn in air by weak politicians?
They came to make our unwise choices wider;
to bleed our aspirations of imagined truths –

to swell the choir with mithering verse?
to heed the clarion of the next futility?
to find their place at Armageddon?

They came in their millions, in total disregard
for paper walls and illegitimate code –
they were just crossing a summer road...

We glanced in the bleak rear-mirror of our facade,
where the fire of four horsemen chased us down.
We were sure we had left all their hooves behind –
except for Death – and the business of souls.

Louder Prayers –
Book Five –

———

A PAGAN PAGEANT

5:1

Remembered on a Frozen Breath

live near the sea
and the sea shouts over the hill at night,
using its laughing voice
to scald the air with healing salt.

The garden is frost and the moon is bright.
I dedicate this quiet truth of cold and night
to everyone – as promised.

5:2

Silence Of Science – Word Of God

God exists, but has gone into hiding;
he understands the basics of familiarity and despair.
Yet the charred text of guarded millennia,
are still rolled-fast in their blind silence.

Their message is safe inside the will of God;
resting in the peaceful hint of a blesséd coming.
A coming by proxy – a utility human –
with a charming charisma, made of astonishing words.

Albeit alone and without a confrère –
and walking on water to smooth his spirit.
It is a fluid path, where he goes as he pleases,
supported by the salt of disciples and gospels.

Yet the universe is built with blocks of silence;
cancelling the need for a god to speak.
God is heard in the quantum infinity,
and in the weak energy of binding light.

Once lit, a religion becomes unstoppably zealous.
And you won't douse its urge
by silence or science.

5 : 3

Comparative Mythologies

No one is listening – no one ever listens.
The oracle performs
only to gauge a standard of betrayal.
But humans are happy – around an old table –
accepting smart comments
favouring social ambition.

The dust soon settles – at least for this evening –
and maybe for tomorrow – until late in the day?
When we wake into the seconds –
trading parcels of moments;
measuring the slow minutes of a final Sun.

Or in a torment of mythologies,
when the Sun becomes a projector –
that great mover of time behind the slenders of dust.
Blending slow mathematics and lyrical sketches,
and the nagging impatience of mysterious song.

It is a sceptical music, chiding riches and beauty,
where we delegate our distances –
to the whereabouts of God.

To the memory of Leonard Cohen

5:4

Steeped In Sunsets

It was photographers
who showed us the final days.
With their millions of images
and their ubiquitous eyes.
And with nothing more left
in their bag of creation,
the end came steeped in sunsets
and their beautiful lies.

   First published on Twitter – 6 September 2021

Words Beyond Death

Writing is a hard machine,
it thumps like a steam hammer, day and night;
echoing in the blood of energised veins
and squeezing out experimental paragraphs of words.
An insistent detective that whittles on,
half-professional, half-paranoid,
as we slump in the interrogation seat of life,
with a light in our face – spilling the beans.

Writing is cat-like too – with feline shapes,
as we play the lines with decisive claws;
unravelling the strands until the ball of ideas
is completely unpicked – spread out like applause.
It teases the presence of each torn letter,
until they look like mercurial shapes of text –
unwound wool, haemorrhaged from tissue;
untitled stories without beginning or end.

We are eternally on call in this radio cosmos –
as are our funeral directors, expecting death.
Dead work – soon veiled from helpless eyes
that might not recognise its stiffened prose.
And certainly not in this unsociable state,
with its illegible message of broken words.

'Words Beyond Death' continues...

They are conveyed in a corpse of paperback deeds,
at the end and beginning of our hardback lives.

We have a notebook too, with a scalpel pen,
so we can cut against its ever-listening skin.
Or test its breath with a bruised mirror,
as solid words fall from the ends of prayers.
They set themselves into a rambling page
where bricks and windows are painted on;
they have no concern for the guiding edge –
the dauntless track of faint blue lines.
It is a tone that might have sweetened the eye
had it not come with a daylight's doubt –
the smothering shuffle of a sunlit curse?

Dead words are better behaved at night.

We have saved ideas in a paper box
or hidden them in our coat of human dust –
unearthed in the prophesy of a day of light
in some dark misery of future years?

In some dark misery of future years,
we will take them out, at long last,

and their shadows will move to light our way
in some reckless balance of life and death.

Later still, we may deny their voice –
those words not caring what they had to say;
while sleeping bereaved, under a seminal breath –
marking the birth of truth into a grieving face.

We are forever at the beck and call of insistence,
and nibbled to the bone by attempts at resistance.
I have left my bed a thousand times
to scribble a truth – into a haunting line –
and they are all somehow enshrined
in the mithering moan of a guiding rhyme.
And also in the mystery of my hinged heart,
where words swing open to the secret hues –
the experimental shades, beyond life's breath,
where the functions of yearning will be deeply profound.

They will torment the spirit into looking back,
where lost words cost nothing in the dimming night.
This sort of commitment, toward our baggaged past,
will reveal its explanations in an eternity of light.

5:6

The Worst That Can Happen

The worst thing that can happen –
is for my poems to have fallen on deaf ears…

"And what about death?
And that they will fade into oblivion?
And isn't that where they belong,
amongst the entropy of the universe?
Amongst the fragmented particles of dark energy?"

If that is where the deaf ears languish, then yes.

     Tycho Brahe – 'Let me not seem to have lived in vain.'

5:7

Thoughts Of Suicide

They never clear my head –
yet are unfit for challenge or reason.
Just to die – is their simple treason –
not so much a message as a qualification.
It is wholly removed from private consideration –
yet perhaps a thing for group conversation?
And the impenetrable chains
of impossible, yet venerable investigation.
For who needs death with its dark exploration
haunting their living ghost.

5:8

Sex Is Plausible

When we are young,
sex is plausible –
almost a career.

Later it becomes
plausibly incurable –
vaguely inscrutable
and possibly forgettable –
sometimes laughable?

Somewhere becoming pain.

To the memory of Philip Larkin

5:9

Apache Rising

Hey Cochise, find Geronimo.
We must attack the Americans once more.
Their Chieftains are losing control
of the plains and the mountains.

August 2021

5:10

Song Of Yourselves

The American skies are darkening
under a deft new wave of politics.
It rolls its cart of modern slogans
to rut the untended White House lawn.

It seems far from the American spirit –
that of binding all the distances –
gathering boundless lakes and oceans
to cradle a home of national courage.

The mighty Mississippi and Missouri
stitch the miles of states and monuments –
a fabric owned by every citizen,
whatever their place in history.

These should be free, within their power,
to symbolise a patriotic stability,
but the two great hearts of America
have grown a culture of sedition.

Their speech is a howling wilderness,
flanked by the banners of identity.
They seep an unnecessary bitterness
into a flag of stated freedoms –

        First published on Twitter – 12 January 2020

Yet this blesséd home for 'leaves of grass'
that stripe the lawns and broken sidewalks –
still spread their stars into the rising foothills
and breathe as one in the wisdom of mountains.

January 2020

5:11

Between Leonards

I saw my son between Leonards –
the living and the darker one.
My son gave me a recording
of Leonard's latest song.
He sang about leaving the table,
he sang himself out of the game.
He said if we want it darker,
he could extinguish the flame.
This was the light that lit my decades;
the light where perception first shone.
By the time I saw my son again
Leonard's light was gone.

On the death of Leonard Cohen:
November 2016

 First published in Fevers of the Mind: October 2021

Victims Of The Black

You are colder than the blasted Sun
that distils its breath into a clouded stare
and chills the wintering, crystal trees
back into the bare leaves of night-filled air.
You are a stark black thing
that has cursed its gold
and left the summer shallows
of the tempered stream –
you have gone deep into old and dark
and everything is black – everything is stark.

Even the spits of airborne ice
that make the seeds of a deeper crop,
are marked for January's sullen grave
that has seized its intake of modern bones.
It has barred our eyes from looking back –

we will not gaze into the black.

I look to the snow – I look to the snow
that has covered the path to my ancient house.
I see my house waist deep – and miles away,
but I cannot get above the lip of ice:
I cannot get above the icy veil.

'Victims of the Black' continues...

I will build another house right here –
this time made of oranges and songs.
It will represent the sunshine you used to fear.

And it is here I will stay – fully lit by your guilt.
Even though everything else is turning grey –
even though everything is moving to black –
and the snow creeping away.

There is a black heart of cruel cold
that tears our fingers into gibbering fools,
and we borrow their skill of tormented black
to wave its blistered hands like claws,
to provide an evidence of probable cause
into the dodging face of our careful killers.

The snowfields are full of murderous minds
and the ominous signs of their shuttered victims.
They show through the ice on these crystal days,
where the cold illustrates an unfortunate path.
It is gleaned by the blood of forensic hearts,
with their unclouded steam of frozen breath;
or the patient clue of over-polished air
that burns the brittle scent of death.

The solid dead have cracked the ice
that pooled beneath the accomplice snow,
and have used these shards to cut their shapes
with wind-assisted geometry.
I have sewn a poultice of rotten leaves
to smother my face in healing black.
It seems unfair to be murdered, but once,
and not be coming back.

5:13

Maurice's Forecast

"It's been a long winter," said Maurice.

"Yes, at least five years," answered Michelle.

"In that case," said Maurice, "we must prepare for winter; the effort of spring is not going well."

5:14

The Death of Miss Detritivore

I saw her by the pool –
lips blooming like forever's lifesaver.
They were feeding gross vanity
to a gathering of souls.
I wandered from their lusty pageant,
but was not saved
by the austerity of my room.

Neither did those lips save beauty –
it was found later in the gloom.
She was anchored to the bottom –
lips downward toward a film of dirt,
meowing her own silence,
like a catfish.

5:15

A Pagan Pageant

Has my country become a pagan state –
having chosen a path of eclectic religion?
Not supporting the word of a single god
but allowing many gods to evolve as a pageant.
An uneasy pantheon, wired to commerce,
or signalling green, as the colour of virtue.

Are we a cabal of regulated mysticism,
involving rare beasts and emotive signs?
The ancient scriptures are retained to appease
those who trust in nothing, lest profound or relic.
Has charity been devised as a plausible miracle –
an interfering panic of commercialised delay?

Some of the gods are lesser-gods now –
considered unworthy by common dissent.
And by the weakening deference of waning interest
that sneaks its whims forward, under simmering stealth.
Are these the sly tools of undermining intolerance
or just the many layers of Hades in the making?

And is this the blank flag of a tenuous administration,
sliding wilfully down the pole of deconstruction?
Sending signals of sunrise to more persistent men –

those employed in the worship of blind intolerance.

They were nurtured with faith, as were we,
but we developed its peace into legislated law.
Yet some loyal, devout and commanded souls
are not easily doused-quiet, or darkly outshone.

Their peace comes with meek and vanquished souls
and the timid apology of the surprised overcome –
an insidious easing, by the subjugation of fools
and the surrendering folly of cowering love.

Some religions are indifferent to adjusting dials;
negotiations are no use to established prophets.
They will not tune in to diverse stations,
to sing with an idealism – given pluralist voice.

Western freedom has lost control
of its freewheeling choice.

Christianity has been cast into the crux of a begging bowl,
via the promiscuous mask of its own eager liberties.
Yet peace shall arise with its persistence of faith –
and advertise Hell – the size of billboards.

A Symbolic Observance Of Amen

I am writing this from my home near the sea,
using invisible ink from the ocean's well.
By the time you read these damp words, they will be dry,
and even more mysterious than they were before –
ingeniously delivered on a blank page –
a blind note, pinned to your door.

You may eventually discover the shapes of these letters,
redrawn by the dry crystals of thriving salt.
As honest a witness as Lot's poor wife –
who turned to look back – as my words do now,
lost in the endurance of an enquiring heart.